SECRETS OF
OUR NATION'S
CAPITAL

SECRETS OF
OUR NATION'S
CAPITAL

WEIRD and
WONDERFUL FACTS
about
WASHINGTON, DC

SUSAN SCHADER LEE

STERLING CHILDREN'S BOOKS
New York

STERLING CHILDREN'S BOOKS
New York

An Imprint of Sterling Publishing
1166 Avenue of the Americas
New York, NY 10036

ISBN 978-1-4549-2003-8

Distributed in Canada by Sterling Publishing Co., Inc.
C/o Canadian Manda Group, 664 Annette Street
Toronto, Ontario, Canada M6S 2C8
Distributed in the United Kingdom by GMC Distribution Services
Castle Place, 166 High Street, Lewes, East Sussex, England BN7 1XU

For information about custom editions, special sales, and premium and corporate purchases, please contact Sterling Special Sales at 800-805-5489 or specialsales@sterlingpublishing.com.

Manufactured in China

Lot #:

2 4 6 8 10 9 7 5 3 1

08/16

www.sterlingpublishing.com

Original illustrations by Jane Sanders

CONTENTS

INTRODUCTION

In 1790, the people of the U.S. government decided that Washington, DC, would be the country's capital city. In 1800, the government moved to its new capital. Government and history attract millions of visitors to the city each year. But there are many reasons to visit this beautiful city! Washington, DC, boasts some of the

country's best museums, beautiful parks, successful sports teams, and more!

In *Secrets Our Nation's Capital* you will find lots of fun facts about this grand city and its treasures. Turn the page to find out what makes Washington, DC, so wonderful!

WASHINGTON, DC

Washington, DC, is the **capital city** of the United States. But that was not always the case! The **government** of the early United States moved around a bit. New York and Philadelphia were both early capitals. Washington, DC, has been home to the U.S. government since 1800.

President George Washington hired **Pierre Charles L'Enfant** to design Washington, DC. L'Enfant was an **architect and a civil engineer**. He created a plan for the city. But he did not listen to the city commissioners and made some bad decisions. The president asked L'Enfant to quit. L'Enfant had wanted $95,500 for the job. In the end, he only earned $3,800!

QUICK
QUIZ

In 1790, government officials decided that Washington, DC, would be the country's capital city. It took many years for Washington, DC, to be planned and built. Government finally moved to Washington in 1800. What city was home to the government from 1790 to 1800?

a) New York   **b)** Philadelphia

c) Boston   **d)** Baltimore

Answer: b

The District of Columbia is not a state, but it has official symbols just as the states do.

Official bird:
Wood Thrush

★ ★ ★

Official tree:
Scarlet Oak

★ ★ ★

Official flower:
American Beauty Rose

Official motto:
Justitia Omnibus, or
Justice for All

★ ★ ★

Official song:
**"The Star-Spangled
Banner"**

★ ★ ★

Official flag:

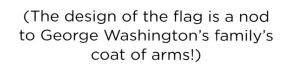

(The design of the flag is a nod
to George Washington's family's
coat of arms!)

DC stands for **"District of Columbia."** The District of Columbia is **not a state**. It is an area of land that belongs to the federal government. The land used to be part of Maryland!

At first, the area for Washington, DC, covered parts of Maryland and Virginia. It was a perfect **diamond shape** of land across the two states. But in 1846, the Virginia side of that land left the district and returned to its home state. This happened for a few reasons. One reason is that the people of Virginia wanted to keep trading slaves. But people were fighting to end the slave trade in Washington, DC. Now, the District of Columbia is an **odd shape**!

How did Washington, DC, get its name? Washington was named for the country's first president, George Washington. The District of Columbia was named for Christopher Columbus. In the late 1700s, Columbia was a popular name for the United States.

Washington, DC, has a carefully planned **street system**. Many streets are named with **letters**. The lettered streets skip over J Street. Why? Some say L'Enfant left out J Street to insult his enemy, chief justice John Jay, who L'Enfant hated. But that is just a **myth**! The real reason there is no J Street is that in the 1700s, the letters *I* and *J* were used as pretty much the **same letter**! Having an I Street and a J street would have been **confusing**.

In 1791, the **first president** of the United States, George Washington, picked a location for the **White House**. But he never lived there! By the time the house was built, Washington was no longer the president. The country's second president, John Adams, moved into the White House in 1800.

Most of the **workers** who built the White House were slaves. Slave owners from Virginia and Maryland were paid $5 a month to loan the people they had enslaved to the project. Trained workers taught many of these people **carpentry skills**. Some of them used their new skills to earn **extra money**.

The White House was not always **white**! The building is made from **sandstone**. For many years the sandstone was not painted. The house was **gray**. After the first reconstruction in 1815–1817, the house was painted white. It takes **570 gallons of paint** to cover the whole house!

The White House you see today is not the same building that President John Adams moved into in 1800. The White House has been **reconstructed** and **renovated** many times. Here are a few of those changes:

1814—The British Army set a fire that destroyed the White House. Reconstruction took two years. The house was not changed during reconstruction.

★ ★ ★

1902—President Theodore Roosevelt began a major renovation. This included adding the West Wing. Now the offices could be kept separate from the home.

★ ★ ★

1909—President William Howard Taft enlarged the presidential office. He also changed the shape from a rectangle to an oval.

1929—An electrical fire on Christmas Eve damaged much of the West Wing. The building was remodeled and the roof was replaced.

★ ★ ★

1933—President Franklin D. Roosevelt was in a wheelchair. He added ramps and modern elevators to the White House so that he could get around. He also added an indoor pool.

★ ★ ★

1948—A close study of the White House revealed that the building was unsafe. It was close to collapsing! The house was completely rebuilt. Only the outer brick walls remained. President Harry S. Truman lived across the street during the four-year project.

Some say the White House is **haunted**! The **ghosts** that have been seen, heard, or smelled include presidents, first ladies, and a president's child. There is a British soldier. There are White House staff members. There is even a cat! The ghost that people sense the most is **President Abraham Lincoln**. He has been seen in rooms all over the White House.

The White House was not always called the White House! It used to be called the **President's Palace**, the **President's House**, or the **Executive Mansion**. President Theodore Roosevelt made the official name the White House in 1901.

At 55,000 square feet, the White House is huge. It is much, much larger than an average house! It includes:

6
levels

★ ★ ★

132
rooms in total

★ ★ ★

35
bathrooms

★ ★ ★

412
doors

★ ★ ★

147
windows

28
fireplaces

★ ★ ★

8
staircases

★ ★ ★

3
elevators

How does this compare with
your home?

What's in the **basement** of the White House? More than just a furnace! The **Situation Room** is a place where the president meets with advisors during a **crisis**. But the basement also has a bowling alley, a flower shop, a carpenter's shop, and a dentist's office!

Many people think the president and family live for **free** at the White House. But that's not true! The first family is expected to pay for its own **meals**, **dry cleaning**, and **toiletries**, such as toothpaste and soap. The president receives a **bill** for those items each month. First families are just like the rest of us!

QUICK QUIZ

Which famous actor bought an espresso machine for the White House's press corps in 2004? He even bought them an updated coffee maker in 2010!

a) Tom Cruise

b) Johnny Depp

c) Tom Hanks

d) Brad Pitt

Answer: c

The White House is the president's **private home**. But it is also open to the public. President Thomas Jefferson first opened the house for **public tours** in the early 1800s. It closes only during times of war. Now, the White House sees 30,000 **visitors** each week! It also receives 65,000 letters, 3,500 phone calls, and 100,000 e-mails each week.

Most presidents have had **pets** live with them at the White House. Dogs and horses are the most popular **presidential pets**. But there have been many **unusual pets**, too. The White House has been home to opossums, a wallaby, a pygmy hippopotamus, and even a hyena!

★ ★ ★

James K. Polk (1845–1849) was the only president who did not keep any pets during his time at the White House.

★ ★ ★

Andrew Johnson (1865–1869) did not have real pets, either, but he took a liking to a family of white mice that hung around his room. He even left out flour for them to eat!

Woodrow Wilson (1913–1921) kept a herd of sheep that grazed on the White House lawn. The ram in the group chewed tobacco!

★ ★ ★

Two presidents had pet alligators. John Quincy Adams (1825–1829) kept his alligator in one of the White House bathrooms. Herbert Hoover's (1929–1933) son sometimes let his two alligators roam freely around the White House grounds!

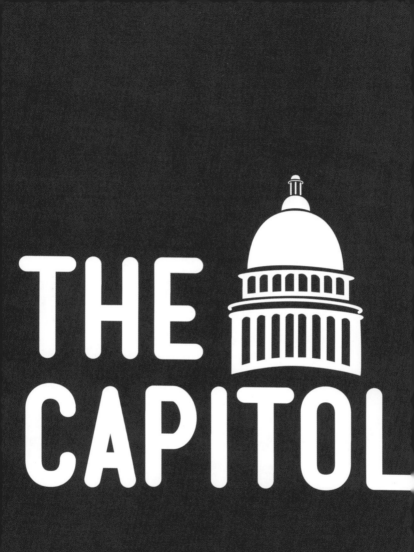

The Capitol is where Congress meets to **vote on new laws**. George Washington laid the **cornerstone** of the Capitol on September 18, 1793. It took **33 years** to complete the building! The original building[*] was not finished until 1826. But Congress first met there on November 17, 1800.

[*]There have been several expansions over the years.

The Capitol is a **massive building** set in the very center of Washington, DC. Here are some of the facts and figures about this impressive building:

The length of the building from north to south is **751 feet**, **4 inches**.

★ ★ ★

The height of the building is **288 feet**.

★ ★ ★

It has **540 rooms**.

★ ★ ★

It has a total of **658 windows**.

★ ★ ★

There are **108 windows** in the dome.

The dome weighs
8,909,200 pounds.

★ ★ ★

The Statue of Freedom
atop the dome weighs
15,000 pounds.

★ ★ ★

The height of the
Statue of Freedom
atop the dome is
19 ½ feet.

During the War of 1812, British troops **set fire** to the Capitol. It almost burned to the ground. But it was **saved** by a storm—the rain put out the fire!

In 1899, the **Height of Buildings Act** was passed. The law stated that no building in Washington, DC, could be taller than the Capitol. By 1910, Congress **changed the law**. Now, there are **four buildings** in the District of Columbia that are taller than the Capitol. These include the Washington Monument, the Basilica of the National Shrine of the Immaculate Conception, the Old Post Office Tower, and the Washington National Cathedral.

The **Architect of the Capitol** is the person who **oversees** the Capitol building and its grounds. The first Architect of the Capitol began the role in 1793. That was more than 220 years ago. But today's Architect of the Capitol is only the eleventh one!

The **National Mall** is a **large park** surrounded by many of the city's important buildings and monuments. Most of them **face inward** toward the park. The Capitol faces outward. This is the case because the Capitol sits on a hill. The side of the building that faces away from the Mall is at ground level. That makes for a **better entrance**.

The shape of the Capitol's National Statuary Hall makes a **whispering gallery**. If you stand in the **right places**, you can hear someone **talking quietly** from many feet away. In fact, you might even hear that person more clearly than you could hear someone talking closer to you!

QUICK QUIZ

There are 100 statues in the National Statuary Hall Collection. Each state in the country has granted the Capitol two statues. Of these 100 statues, how many are of women?

a) 48   **b)** 13

c) 26   **d)** 9

Answer: d

People claim to see a **ghost cat** in the basement of the Capitol. The cat is usually seen in the **hall** between the crypt and the Old Supreme Court Chamber. In fact, visitors have reported seeing actual **paw prints** pressed into the stone floor!

In 1887, a reporter wrote an **article** about a congressman that made the congressman **angry**. Three years later, the congressman saw the reporter near some stairs in the Capitol. The reporter took out a gun and shot the congressman. The congressman died a few days later. The stairs still have **bloodstains**. Many people claim that the congressman's **ghost** walks up and down the stairs!

In the crypt, a bust of **President Abraham Lincoln** is on display. But the sculptor, Gutzon Borglum, gave Lincoln **only one ear**! Borglum believed that during the Civil War, Lincoln listened only to the northern states and not to the southern ones. He meant for Lincoln's one ear to face north. But because of the bust's position, the ear actually faces south!

When President George Washington died, Congress wanted to **honor** him by burying him in the Capitol. They built a **tomb** under the crypt. But President Washington's will stated that he wanted to be **buried at his home**. Indeed, he was buried at Mount Vernon. But the space for the tomb is still in the basement of the Capitol today!

The Capitol has its own **subway**! Beginning in 1909, subways were added to the Capitol's basement. They are still there today. The trains **carry people** between the Capitol and the offices for the House of Representatives and the Senate. But you need a staff ID to **ride** the trains.

There are two **marble bathtubs** in the basement of the Capitol! Several marble bathtubs were installed in 1859. At the time, most senators had **no running water** at home. That made taking a bath harder. The baths in the Capitol made it easier for senators to stay clean. By the 1890s, most senators lived in homes with running water. Most of the bathtubs were removed. But two **still remain**!

NATIONAL
ARCHIVES

The National Archives holds the **records** for the **entire country**! It keeps a wide variety of documents. The documents form a record of our country's history. Some of the types of documents in the National Archives are:

- ✔ records of slavery
- ✔ military records
- ✔ records of exploration expeditions
- ✔ Native American treaties
- ✔ records about land purchases
- ✔ census records
- ✔ presidential inaugural addresses
- ✔ records of Supreme Court cases

QUICK
QUIZ

Congress created the National Archives in 1934, but many of the records in the Archives are older than that. What year do the records date back to?

a) 1620

b) 1775

c) 1865

d) 1914

Answer: b

The National Archives stores some of the **most important documents** from our country's history. Many of them have been **digitized**. You can find them on the Internet at www.ourdocuments.gov! These are some of the documents on the site:

- ✓ Declaration of Independence
- ✓ Constitution
- ✓ Bill of Rights
- ✓ Louisiana Purchase Treaty
- ✓ Emancipation Proclamation
- ✓ Gettysburg Address
- ✓ Documents related to the Supreme Court case *Brown v. Board of Education*

The National Archives keeps only records that they think will **have value** in the future. This means they keep only a **small portion** of all that is created. The Archives keeps about 2 to 5 percent of records each year. Still, things add up! The National Archives contains:

10 billion
pages of
textual records

★ ★ ★

12 million
maps, charts, and architectural
and engineering drawings

★ ★ ★

25 million
still photographs
and graphics

24 million
aerial photographs

★ ★ ★

300,000
reels of motion picture film

★ ★ ★

400,000
video and
sound recordings

★ ★ ★

133 terabytes
of electronic data

These numbers do not include
the large numbers of records in other
locations across the country. These
are just the numbers at the main
Archives in Washington, DC.
It's a lot to keep track of!

Word Search

The National Archives includes presidential libraries. Thirteen presidents have libraries. Find their names in the word search. (Note that there are only 12 names below. That's because George H. W. Bush and George W. Bush BOTH have libraries.)

```
B T E G H B B X Y F D J L F J
H H L S I C X S D G N E T G T
W O U E A X F Q E C R P R N U
Z B O R V C L I N T O N U W K
C J T V N E C U N X E U M I H
A E M D E O S G E B W X A P M
R O Y H A R X O K E V W N D R
N A G A E R X I O D B C I T N
O P D U K M O L N R T U W O F
Z Z Z C R U W L X Q V K S D U
W B K C M R C L H V F N N R W
R E W O H N E S I E H A I O N
C T V Z Z O K U L O X L L F N
W A M A N Y M A J X Z V V H P
B J K P L J C J R J K C X J J
```

BUSH	FORD	NIXON
CARTER	HOOVER	REAGAN
CLINTON	JOHNSON	ROOSEVELT
EISENHOWER	KENNEDY	TRUMAN

Check the answer key on page 158 to see the completed word search.

Government records are in the public domain. This means that they belong to the public. There are some records in the National Archives that may have a copyright. But mostly, the records are open for the people to use freely! Anyone may view them, print text or images in books, and so on.

The Library of Congress is the **national library** of the United States. Anyone 16 years and older may use the **library's collections**. But people may not check out the books! The library is not a **lending library**. Only members of Congress and their staffs may check out the books.

The **Library of Congress** opened in the Capitol building in 1800. When the British set the Capitol on fire in 1814, the library's **collection burned**, too. The fire **destroyed** about 3,000 books. But the library was quick to **rebuild** its collection. Just five months later, the library bought 6,487 books from Thomas Jefferson! Jefferson earned $23,950 for the lot.

The **Librarian of Congress** is in charge of the Library of Congress. The president of the United States chooses the Librarian. The Senate votes to approve the president's choice. The **current Librarian** is the 14th one since the Library opened in 1800! He has held the role since 2015.

The Library of Congress is the **largest library in the entire world**! Just how big is it? The truth is in the numbers!

Nearly 3,200
staff members

★ ★ ★

More than 1.6 million
visitors each year

★ ★ ★

838 miles
of bookshelves

★ ★ ★

160 million
items in the collections

★ ★ ★

37 million
books and other print materials

3.5 million
recordings

★ ★ ★

14 million
photographs

★ ★ ★

5.5 million
maps

★ ★ ★

7.1 million
pieces of sheet music

★ ★ ★

69 million
manuscripts

How can one library **store** such a large collection of materials? The Library of Congress is **spread across three buildings**. Underground passageways connect the three buildings. The Library also has two off-site storage locations in nearby Maryland.

QUICK
QUIZ

Only about half of the book and serial collections in the Library of Congress are in English. About how many other languages are found in the other half?

a) 470

b) 60

c) 330

d) 120

Answer: a

The **smallest book** in the Library's collection is a 1985 version of *Old King Cole*. The book is just 1/25 inch × 1/25 inch. That's smaller than your **fingernail**!

The **largest book** in the Library's collection is about the Southeast Asian country Bhutan. A group of American students photographed Bhutan's ancient way of life. They put the photos together in a book that is 5 feet × 7 feet. That's **taller than most adults**!

The Library of Congress may date back only to 1800, but its collections go much **farther back**. The library's **oldest written** work is a cuneiform tablet. A wedge-shaped reed was used to carve the writing into a clay tablet. The library's **oldest tablet** is from 2040 BCE!

The Library of Congress has the world's **largest collection of maps**. There are 5.5 million items in the collection. One of these is a **world map** by Martin Waldseemüller. The map is from the year 1507. It is the **first time** the name *America* was written.

America's Birth Certificate

MONUMENTS
AND MEMORIALS

There are many **monuments and memorials** scattered across Washington, DC. But the most famous live on the **National Mall**. The National Mall is a large, grassy park. It is sometimes called "America's Front Yard," because it lies in front of the White House. There are nine monuments and memorials on the Mall:

Washington Monument (dedicated in 1885)

Lincoln Memorial (dedicated in 1922)

DC War Memorial (World War I) (dedicated in 1931)

Thomas Jefferson Memorial (dedicated in 1943)

Vietnam Veterans Memorial (dedicated in 1982)

Korean War Veterans Memorial (dedicated in 1995)

Franklin Delano Roosevelt Memorial (dedicated in 1997)

World War II Memorial (dedicated in 2004)

Martin Luther King, Jr. Memorial (dedicated in 2011)

George Washington once got in the way of his **own monument**! The Continental Congress wanted to build a **statue of Washington** in 1783 because of his role in the Revolutionary War. Once he became president, he ended the project because government funds were tight.

If you look closely, you'll notice that the Washington Monument is **two different colors**. In July 1848, the cornerstone of the monument was laid. But the project stalled in 1854 and wasn't finished until 1879. At that later time, the builders used marble from a **different quarry**. The two types of marble looked the same at first, but they have **weathered differently** over time. Now the bottom 150 feet is one color and the rest of the monument is another.

When it was **finished** in 1884, the Washington Monument was the **tallest structure** in the world! Soon afterward, though, the **Eiffel Tower** in Paris topped it. Since then, many taller buildings have been built. But the Washington Monument remains the tallest structure in Washington, DC. Let's look at the numbers:

Height of the monument:
555 feet, 5 $\frac{1}{8}$ inches

★ ★ ★

Height of the observation deck:
500 feet

★ ★ ★

Height of the museum: **490 feet**

★ ★ ★

The number of steps within the monument:
897

The number of seconds
it takes to ride the elevator
to the observation deck:

70

★ ★ ★

Width of base:

55 feet

★ ★ ★

The number of stones used
to build the monument:

36,000

★ ★ ★

Weight of the monument
(with the underground
foundation included):

100,000 tons

★ ★ ★

The number of
visitors each year:

800,000

QUICK

QUIZ

What shape is the Washington Monument?

a) column

b) cylinder

c) obelisk

d) pyramid

Answer: c

In 2011, Washington, DC, shook from a **rare earthquake**. The earthquake measured 5.8 on the Richter scale. It was enough to cause **major damage** to the Washington Monument. The monument had to close down. It took 500 tons of scaffolding, $15 million, and three years to reopen the monument!

An **architect** named Henry Bacon designed the Lincoln Memorial. Bacon based his design on the **Parthenon** in Athens, Greece. Why did Bacon base his design on an ancient Greek temple? Because Lincoln fought for **democracy**, and democracy began in Greece.

The **Lincoln Memorial** is made from a number of different stones. The stones come from all over the country: **granite** from Massachusetts, **limestone** from Indiana, and different types of **marble** from Colorado, Tennessee, Alabama, and Georgia. Henry Bacon had a reason for **mixing stones**. He wanted the memorial to show that different parts of the country can work together.

The Lincoln Memorial is a grand sight! Let's look at the numbers:

Width of the Lincoln statue: 19 feet

★ ★ ★

Height of the Lincoln statue: 19 feet

★ ★ ★

Weight of the Lincoln statue: 120 tons

★ ★ ★

Weight of the Lincoln statue with the pedestal: 175 tons

★ ★ ★

Width of the statue's head: 2 feet, 7 inches

★ ★ ★

Height of the statue's head: 3 feet, 7 inches

Length of the full memorial: **201 feet**

★ ★ ★

Width of the full memorial: **132 feet**

★ ★ ★

Height of the full memorial: **99 feet**

★ ★ ★

Weight of the full memorial:
38,000 tons

The Lincoln statue originally was going to be only 10 feet tall. The 19-foot statue is nearly double that! It is so big that if Lincoln were to stand up, he would be 28 feet tall!

There are **36 columns** lined up around the outside of the Lincoln Memorial. They number 36 because there were 36 states in the Union when President Lincoln died. The columns look like they stand **straight up and down**. But they don't! They actually **lean inward** a bit. The reason for this is to avoid an **optical illusion** that would make the memorial look asymmetrical.

On one wall of the Lincoln Memorial, Lincoln's **Second Inaugural Address** is carved into the stone. But it was cut with a **spelling mistake**! At the end of the first paragraph, the word *FUTURE* was spelled *EUTURE*! It was fixed, but if you look closely, you can still see the bottom part of the *E* there.

Martin Luther King, Jr. was an African American civil rights **activist**. He fought for all people to have **equal rights** no matter what their race. He gave his famous "I Have a Dream" speech from the steps of the Lincoln Memorial.

The **DC War Memorial** is different from the rest of the memorials on the National Mall. The DC War Memorial is **not a national monument**. It honors DC citizens who served in World War I. In fact, there is no national memorial dedicated to World War I in the District of Columbia! Some members of Congress are fighting to make the DC War Memorial a national memorial.

The Thomas Jefferson Memorial has a **familiar shape**. It looks similar to the ancient Pantheon building in Rome, Italy. But it is also **modeled** after the Rotunda at the University of Virginia. Thomas Jefferson himself designed the Rotunda!

Hidden within the stone of the Thomas Jefferson Memorial is a **time capsule**! There are **several newspapers** from 1939 and some of Jefferson's writings. There is even a copy of the Declaration of Independence and a copy of the U.S. Constitution inside the stone!

QUICK QUIZ

Many people opposed the building of the Thomas Jefferson Memorial. Which of the below is NOT a reason people didn't want it to be built?

a) Some people did not think Thomas Jefferson had been a good president.

b) Some people were worried that the view of the Potomac River would be ruined.

c) Some modern architects did not like the classical design.

d) Some people were upset that many cherry trees would be chopped down to make room for the memorial.

Answer: a

The Thomas Jefferson Memorial was dedicated on April 13, 1943. It would have been Jefferson's 200th birthday. At the time, the memorial was not actually complete! The 19-foot statue of Jefferson had to be cast in plaster, because metals were rationed during World War II. People could only get a limited amount. In 1947, the plaster statue was replaced with the bronze statue.

The Vietnam Veterans Memorial is made from **black granite**. It is a very simple wall, with the names of over 58,000 soldiers who died in the Vietnam War. Many people were **unhappy with this design**. Therefore, two years after the wall was dedicated, a statue of three servicemen and the U.S. flag was added. Nine years later, another statue was added. This one is of three women caring for an injured soldier.

The Vietnam Veterans Memorial was built without government money! A Vietnam veteran named Jan C. Scruggs **started a fund** with $2,800 of his own money. Many famous people helped with **fund-raising**. The efforts were a success. Altogether, Scruggs's fund raised $8.4 million!

Names are still being added to the Vietnam Veterans Memorial decades later! Sometimes veterans' deaths can be linked to the **wounds** they got in the war. There are also some names on the wall of people who **survived** the war—oops!

The Korean War Veterans Memorial is **another memorial** that is very different from the classical white marble and limestone buildings. It is the **first memorial** in Washington, DC, to be made from **stainless steel**! Nineteen stainless steel statues of soldiers stand among granite strips and juniper bushes.

The **statues** at the Korean War Veterans Memorial are **reflected** in a black granite wall. The 164-foot-long wall is covered in **photographic images**. They were sandblasted onto the wall! A computer created a stencil from photographs of the war. Then the stencil guided the sandblasting to carve the images into the wall.

The Franklin Delano Roosevelt Memorial is the **biggest presidential memorial** on the National Mall. It has statues tucked into **quiet spaces**, **trees**, and **waterfalls**. It feels like a hidden garden. But it actually spans 7.5 acres!

Roosevelt once said that he would want a **memorial** for him to be no bigger than his desk. At first, Congress followed his request. But they felt it was not enough to honor such an **important man**. Roosevelt was the only president to be elected to more than two terms—he was elected **four times**! And he led the country through the Great Depression AND World War II. So Congress built the current memorial instead.

The Franklin Delano Roosevelt Memorial includes 10 **bronze sculptures**. One of these is of First Lady Eleanor Roosevelt. It is the only presidential memorial to include a **first lady**. There is also a statue of Roosevelt's dog, Fala! Fala is the only **presidential pet** ever to be included in a memorial.

The Franklin Delano Roosevelt Memorial is the first memorial in Washington, DC, to be fully **wheelchair accessible**! After getting a disease called polio, Roosevelt had to use a wheelchair. Therefore, it is fitting that his memorial be accomodating to people who use wheelchairs.

The World War II Memorial was not built from scratch. The **Rainbow Pool** is a small pool right next to the Lincoln Memorial Reflecting Pool. It was built in the early 1920s. The World War II Memorial was planned around the Rainbow Pool!

QUICK
QUIZ

The politician Bob Dole led a fund-raising campaign to build the World War II Memorial. Which famous actor led the campaign with him?

a) Tom Cruise   **b)** Johnny Depp

c) Tom Hanks   **d)** Brad Pitt

Answer: c

The **World War II Memorial** honors all of the Americans who served in World War II. There were 16 million people in the American armed forces during that war! More than 400,000 Americans died in the war. The **Freedom Wall** is part of the memorial that honors the lives lost. There are 4,048 **gold stars** on the wall. Each star stands for 100 lives.

QUICK
QUIZ

The deadliest war for U.S. soldiers killed 620,000 Americans. Can you guess which war this was?

a) Revolutionary War

b) Civil War

c) World War I

d) Vietnam War

Answer: b

During World War II, there was a bit of **graffiti** that was popular with American troops. It was a cartoon of a **man peeking over a wall**. American soldiers drew the cartoon and wrote "Kilroy was here" before leaving an area. The World War II Memorial includes two Kilroy engravings. But they are hidden, so you have to search for them!

The **Martin Luther King, Jr. Memorial** is the first memorial in Washington, DC, that **honors an African American**. But the memorial is actually of Chinese origin! Chinese artist Lei Yixin sculpted the memorial from Chinese granite. He even did the work in China.

The Martin Luther King, Jr. Memorial is surrounded by **cherry blossom trees**. The trees **blossom** in early spring. Usually the peak is around April 4. That is also the date when King was killed.

The address of the
Martin Luther King, Jr.
Memorial has meaning.
The Memorial lives at 1964
Independence Avenue.
The address is a nod to the
1964 Civil Rights Act. The
Act made discriminating
against people because of
their race, sex, or religion
against the law. Martin
Luther King, Jr. was key in
helping to pass the law.

The **entrance** to the Martin Luther King, Jr. Memorial is made of two **giant stones**. Standing a bit in front of the stones is a **powerful** 30-foot statue of King. Surrounding the stones and statue is a 450-foot wall covered in 16 quotes from King.

THE 🖌

SMITHSONIAN

INSTITUTION

The **Smithsonian Institution** was founded in 1846. It is a group of 19 museums and galleries, 9 research centers, and a zoo. Its **goal** is to help the world learn and share knowledge. It is the **largest complex** of this kind. All but two museums are in the United States. Most of the Smithsonian is in Washington, DC.

The entire Smithsonian Institution was once **housed in one building**. Now the Smithsonian's collections are housed in **many buildings**. There are about 138 million works of art, artifacts, and specimens in the complete collection! The Smithsonian saves everything from astronaut boots to insect eggs to old advertisements.

Word Search

The Smithsonian Institution's museums and research centers cover many subjects. They span art, science, and history. Find the words below in the word search.

```
S  P  M  P  N  O  N  V  V  V  J  B  I  S  Y
M  T  U  O  O  N  U  A  V  I  D  B  T  W  R
A  M  E  R  I  C  A  N  T  R  P  C  H  E  Q
H  P  S  T  T  E  R  N  A  I  A  X  S  U  J
X  D  U  R  C  Q  J  V  Z  F  O  E  O  P  M
D  X  M  A  E  F  N  M  I  Q  A  N  A  P  Y
Y  P  K  I  L  R  G  T  Z  R  J  S  A  O  D
C  R  J  T  L  P  R  F  C  J  D  S  W  L  S
R  U  O  B  O  A  H  H  Y  R  E  L  L  A  G
J  J  N  T  C  O  E  M  E  X  Q  R  C  S  I
M  J  E  H  S  R  T  C  A  R  T  Z  L  K  S
P  B  J  Q  W  I  A  R  P  B  F  W  O  M  D
E  Q  O  D  N  P  H  J  P  C  O  E  Q  O  R
B  H  O  H  S  Z  G  S  X  F  Q  M  D  K  W
Q  J  W  J  Z  C  S  Z  C  I  L  N  L  M  O
```

AMERICAN	GALLERY	PORTRAIT
ART	HISTORY	RESEARCH
ARTIFACTS	MUSEUM	SPACE
COLLECTION	NATIONAL	ZOO

Check the answer key on page 158 to see the completed word search.

The Smithsonian Institution has an **interesting mix** of items in its collection. It includes one of President Truman's bowling pins, Dorothy's ruby slippers from the movie *The Wizard of Oz*, dinosaur poop, locks of hair from early presidents, and a carrier pigeon from World War I!

The Smithsonian's National Air and Space Museum opened on the National Mall in 1976. The museum's collection is made up of almost **60,000 objects**. The collection ranges from **microchips** to **space helmets** to **jet airplanes** to **rockets**. It is the largest of its kind in the world!

The Smithsonian's National Museum of American History opened on the National Mall in 1964. The collection covers everything from **politics** to **pop culture** to **science** and **technology**. It goes right back to the beginnings of our country's history. In 1620, Pilgrims landed at Plymouth Rock. Two pieces of the **famous rock** are among the museum's artifacts. The larger piece weighs 100 pounds!

The Smithsonian's National Museum of Natural History opened on the National Mall in 1910. In addition to natural history, the museum included history, technology, and art. In 1957, the museum was split into separate museums. The National Museum of Natural History remained in the original location. It keeps more than 127 million specimens and artifacts!

Many Smithsonian museums are on the **National Mall**. The National Portrait Gallery and the American Art Museum are not. The building that houses them has a **lot of history** though! They are in the old U.S. Patent Office building. That building also served as a barracks and a hospital for wounded soldiers during the **Civil War**.

The Smithsonian's **National Zoo** opened in 1889. About 1,800 animals from about 300 different species live at the zoo. Almost a quarter of them are **endangered species**. The zoo's most popular endangered animals are their giant pandas. You can even watch the pandas 24/7 on the zoo's live webcam!

MUSEUMS, HISTORIC SITES, PARKS, AND WATERWAYS

A large number of the museums in Washington, DC, are part of the Smithsonian Institution. But not all of them! There are many other outstanding museums to check out.

At the **Bureau of Engraving and Printing**, you can see where U.S. paper money is made! You'll learn that currency paper is made of $\frac{3}{4}$ cotton and $\frac{1}{4}$ linen. Take a tour to see where **millions of dollars** are being printed. The Bureau has a location in Washington, DC, and another one in Fort Worth, TX. Together, the two print billions of dollars each year.

QUICK
QUIZ

Which of the following is the first woman ever to have her portrait appear on U.S. paper money?

a) Dolly Madison

b) Eleanor Roosevelt

c) Susan B. Anthony

d) Martha Washington

Answer: d

The International Spy Museum follows the **history of espionage** from biblical times to today! Stories of real spies and their missions show how they have affected important historical moments. The museum spotlights the largest collection of **spy artifacts** ever put on display. It has everything from concealment devices and sabotage weapons to cipher machines and microdots.

The U.S. Holocaust Museum memorializes the **tragedy** of the Holocaust. It aims to **confront hatred** across the world. There are two large milk cans buried at the museum site. The cans hold soil and ashes from concentration camps. More than 90 Holocaust survivors **volunteer** at the museum. They are glad to share their **personal stories** of the horrible history to visitors.

The oldest building in Washington, DC, is called the **Old Stone House**. It was built in 1765. That's before the United States had even formed! The blue granite building still stands on its **original foundation**. In fact, 85 percent of the building is still original construction from the 1700s! The U.S. government bought it in 1953. Now the National Park Service maintains the house as a historic site.

Clara Barton was an **important nurse** during the Civil War. The home where she lived during that time still stands in Washington, DC. It is now called The Clara Barton Missing Soldiers Office Museum. Why? After working on the battlefield, Barton helped **track down** missing soldiers. She **uncovered** the fate of 22,000 soldiers!

Frederick Douglass **escaped slavery** early in his life. He then dedicated himself to fighting for justice for all people. He spent the last years of his life living at Cedar Hill in Washington, DC. The National Park Service adopted Cedar Hill in 1962. Today you can **tour the home** to see how Frederick Douglass lived. Seventy percent of the artifacts are original!

Frederick Douglass's home at Cedar Hill had between six and fourteen rooms when it was built in the late 1850s. Douglass added more rooms for a total of 21. Still, sometimes Douglass felt the need for **more privacy**. For that, he had a small stone cabin behind the house. The cabin was called a **Growlery**. It had a fireplace, a desk, and a couch.

Just three miles from the White House is a **hilltop house**. It has been called a cottage, but it is far from small. The cottage has 34 rooms! Four presidents used the cottage as a **summer home**. Abraham Lincoln used it for three summers during the Civil War. He wrote the final draft of the Emancipation Proclamation there.

President Abraham Lincoln was **assassinated** at Ford's Theatre on April 14, 1865. The National Park Service took over the building in 1932. They **rebuilt** it to look as it did in 1865. Visitors can see what the theater looked like when Lincoln was shot, though nothing inside is original. But the **exterior walls** are still the ones from the 1800s!

QUICK
QUIZ

Ford's Theatre has a long history of being a theater, but that wasn't always the case! What was the building before it was a theater?

a) a grocery   **b)** a hotel

c) a post office   **d)** a church

Answer: d

Many people know that Abraham Lincoln was assassinated at **Ford's Theatre**. But he did not actually die there. After he was shot, he was moved to a **boarding house** across the street. Lincoln was too tall for the bed, and had to be laid down **diagonally**! The Petersen House is still there. The National Park Service keeps the historic site open as a museum.

The United States National Arboretum is a 446-acre **public garden**. Visitors enjoy many kinds of **trees**, **shrubs**, and **flowers**. But it is also a **research center**. The arboretum works to form new breeds of plants that are hardier. Researchers have created over 650 new types of plants!

Visitors to the National Arboretum expect to see **lots of plants**. But they will also see **22 columns** from a building standing on the grounds. The columns look like they have been part of the arboretum's grounds for a very long time. But they were **added** only a few decades ago. The columns were originally part of the Capitol building!

Rock Creek Park is a 1,754-acre park in the northern part of Washington, DC. It opened in 1890 as a national park. It has **woodsy hiking trails** and **human-made playgrounds**. People bike, hike, and play golf in the park. They also  rent boats and ride horses. The park even has its own **planetarium**!

Word Search

Rock Creek Park is full of wildlife. Find some of the animals hidden in the word search.

```
D S R J Z T K T D W M U A H M
T R N D D M N S O Y U T O T J
I E J H J Q M O T M X G X V P
B V C Q I Y D W Q V L G O A N
U A I S U P B H P C T W A F T
K E I L E R R I U Q S E O R N
T B N C R C Z U D H T E L Y V
A T K O R T F G J O D J K N B
B E U O O U P Q Y R A B B I T
R Y W R R C N O K G X M Q G C
W F W P T M C H B A O A B V W
B G D G V L W A B I H T E K G
J W E T A S E Y R L N X M L U
Q E E C W M R T W W J X O F N
K Y R G P A Y H O Z Q S B O D
```

BAT	DEER	RACCOON
BEAVER	FOX	SQUIRREL
COYOTE	OWL	TURTLE
CROW	RABBIT	WOODPECKER

Check the answer key on page 158 to
see the completed word search.

From 1828 to 1924, the Chesapeake and Ohio Canal was used to **transport coal and other goods** to communities from Cumberland, MD, down to Washington, DC. The canal and its towpath became the C&O National Historical Park in 1971. The canal is no longer active. Now it is used as a place to **enjoy nature** and learn some local history!

There are several **gold mines** in the Great Falls area of the C&O National Historical Park! Gold was first **discovered** there by a Union soldier during the Civil War.

Building the Chesapeake and Ohio Canal was quite a project! Let's look at the numbers.

Length of the canal: **184.5 miles**

★ ★ ★

Depth of the canal: **2 to 6 feet**

★ ★ ★

Width of the canal: **60 to 80 feet**

★ ★ ★

Width of the towpath (which runs alongside the canal): **7 to 12 feet**

★ ★ ★

Numbers of total laborers who dug the canal and built its aqueducts, culverts, locks, and lock houses: **30,000**

★ ★ ★

The highest number of laborers working at one time: **4,000**

★ ★ ★

The length of time it took to build the canal (1828–1850): **22 years**

The cost to build the canal: $14 million

★ ★ ★

Number of boats that worked on the canal at the peak of its usage: 500

★ ★ ★

Length of a journey down the canal (assuming 18 hours per day of travel): 5 to 7 days

★ ★ ★

Speed limit for boats: 4 mph

★ ★ ★

Weight of coal carried in each boat: 100 to 120 tons

★ ★ ★

Amount a boat earned for carrying 100 tons of coal: $25

How did the boats on the Chesapeake and Ohio Canal move? They were **pulled by mules**! Two sets of two to three mules were assigned to each boat. When it was time to go, the mules were tied to the boat, then walked on the towpath alongside the canal. The boat got pulled right along!

The Tidal Basin is a **human-made inlet** between the Potomac River and the National Mall. It is a **beautiful** place that people enjoy. You can stroll around the outside of the basin or rent a paddleboat for a ride on the water. There are **grand views** of many of the Mall's memorials. But the Tidal Basin was created with a purpose, too! It drains the Washington Channel after a high tide.

QUICK
QUIZ

Several memorials sit right next to the basin. Which memorial is NOT on the basin's border?

a) Thomas Jefferson Memorial

b) Abraham Lincoln Memorial

c) Martin Luther King, Jr. Memorial

d) Franklin Delano Roosevelt Memorial

Answer: b

Thousands of cherry trees are planted around the Tidal Basin. They were a gift from Tokyo, Japan, to Washington, DC, in 1912. The 3,020 trees represented the friendship between the two cities. But this was actually the second attempt at a cherry tree gift. In 1910, Tokyo sent 2,000 cherry trees to Washington. But the trees arrived infested with insects and diseases, and they had to be burned!

The **original gift** of 3,020 cherry trees included 12 different varieties of trees! Eighteen hundred of the trees were Yoshino cherry trees. During a **small ceremony**, the first two Yoshinos were planted on the northern bank of the Tidal Basin. These two trees still stand there today!

The cherry trees around Washington, DC, **bloom** from mid-March to mid-April. Once they do, the city **celebrates** the beginning of spring with the National Cherry Blossom Festival. The **yearly festival** began in 1935. Today's festival lasts for several weeks. It includes a parade, a kite-flying competition, fireworks, music and dance performances, and more!

PROFESSIONAL SPORTS

Word Search

Washington, DC, is home to seven professional sports teams. Find the names of the sports and the teams in the word search.

```
Q T S W J L N I K G U L S B S
B A S K E T B A L L K I U A C
B I I N J X S K T U J N Y S I
E W Y D I D E I P I I K B E T
D F R D R K J L O T O A E B S
N W P A G H S C E R X N H A Y
L N Z U X B A D R L P I A L M
F I G E O P P B E J P B J L N
W C B F I T H L Y R U I S V S
X X D T H F C O O L Q I O P E
D B A D Q V E O C M F L C O L
R L E F C B D H X K Q S C Y I
S M C J O R F Z B H E K E U U
L L A B T O O F A R V Y R I Q
S P O R T S B C N J F Q B P K
```

BASEBALL	HOCKEY	SOCCER
BASKETBALL	MYSTICS	SPORTS
CAPITALS	NATIONALS	UNITED
FOOTBALL	REDSKINS	WIZARDS

Check the answer key on page 158 to see the completed word search.

The Washington Redskins actually began in Boston under the name the **Boston Braves**! They changed their name to the **Boston Redskins** the following year. But they never gained a strong fan base in Boston. So in 1937, the team moved to Washington. They have been Washington's most popular sports team for decades.

The Washington Redskins' **home stadium** is not actually in Washington at all. It is located in Landover, Maryland. FedEx Field was once  the largest stadium in the National Football League, with 91,704 seats!

Washington, DC's **professional baseball team** is the Washington Nationals. But the Nationals are **quite new** to the city. The Montreal Expos moved from Canada to Washington, DC, in 2005. Before that, the District of Columbia had no baseball team for 34 years!

Which baseball team did Washington locals root for during the 34 years when the city did not have its own team?

a) Philadelphia Phillies

b) Pittsburgh Pirates

c) Baltimore Orioles

d) New York Mets

Answer: c

Washington, DC's professional men's basketball team is the Washington Wizards. The team has been through **many cities** and **many team names**. It settled in Washington, DC, in 1973. At the time, the team was called the Bullets. But the owners thought it sounded too violent. So in 1995, they set out to choose a **new name**. The team's owner set up a naming contest in Washington, DC. "Wizards" was the winner!

The Washington Mystics is the Dictrict of Columbia's professional **women's basketball** team. Their team mascot is **Pax the Panda**. It is based on the popularity of the pandas at the National Zoo!

Major League Soccer (MLS) in North America is **relatively new**. It began as recently as the mid-1990s. The first team in the League was given to Washington, DC! The team is called **DC United**, and they have won the secondmost trophies of any team in the MLS.

QUICK
QUIZ

The soccer team DC United plays its home games at the RFK Stadium. Many other professional sports teams have called the historic stadium "home." Which team has NOT played at RFK Stadium?

a) Washington Wizards (basketball)

b) Washington Redskins (football)

c) Washington Senators (baseball)

d) Washington Nationals (baseball)

Answer: a

The Washington Capitals has been the professional **ice hockey** team in Washington, DC, since 1974. For the first 21 seasons, the team colors were a patriotic combination: **red, white, and blue**.

In 1995, the team colors changed to **blue, black, and gold**. Their logo was also changed to a fierce bald eagle with sharp talons. The combination of the new logo with the new colors was meant to give the team a **bolder** feel on the ice.

But the new colors did not last long! In 2007, the Capitals returned to their roots. They got rid of the aggressive-looking eagle logo. They also brought back the original red, white, and blue colors for a more **traditional** feel.

ANSWER KEY

PAGE 56

```
B T E G H B B X Y F D J L F J
H H L S I C X S D G N E T G T
W O U E A X F Q E C R P T N U
Z B O R V C L I N T O N U W K
C J T V N E C U N X E U M I H
A E M D E O S G E B W X A P M
R O Y H A R X O K E V V W N D R
N A G A E R X I O D B C I T N
O P D U K M O L N R T U W O F
Z Z Z C R U W L X Q V K S D U
W B K C M R C L H V F N N R W
R E W O H N E S I E H A I O N
C T V Z Z O K U L O X L F N
W A M A N Y M A J X Z V V H P
B J K P L J C J R J K C X J J
```

PAGE 111

```
S P M P N O N V V V J B I S Y
M T U O O N U A V I D B T W R
A M E R I C A N T R P C H E Q
H P S T T E R N A I A X S U J
X D U R C Q J V Z F O E O P M
D X M A E F N M I G A N A P Y
Y R J T L P R F C J D S W L S
C R U O B O A H H Y R E L L A G
J J N T C O E M E X Q R C S I
M J E H S R T C A R T Z L K S
P B J Q W I A R P B F W O M D
E Q O D N P P C O E Q O X
B H O H S Z G S X F Q M D K W
Q J W J Z C S Z C I L N L M O
```

PAGE 135

```
D S R J Z T K T D W M U A H M
T R N D D M N S O Y U T O T J
I E J H J Q M O T M X G X V P
B V C Q I Y D W Q V L G O A N
U A I S U P B H P C T W A F T
K E I L E R R I U Q S E O R N
T B N C R C Z U D H T E L Y V
A T K O R T F G J O D J K N B
B E U O O U P Q Y R A B B I T
R Y W R R C N O K G X M Q G C
W F W P T M C H B A O A B V W
B G D G V L W A B I H T E K G
J W E T A S E Y R L N X M L U
Q E E C W M R T W W J X O F N
K Y R G P A Y H O Z Q S B O D
```

PAGE 147

```
Q T S W J L N I K G U L S B
B A S K E T B A L L K I U A C
B I I N J X S K T U J N Y S I
E W Y D I D E I P I X K E B T
D F R D R K J L O T O A E S Y
N W P A G H S C E R X N H A M
L N Z U X B A D R L P I A L N
F I G E O P P B E J P A L N S
W C B F I T H L Y R U I S V S
X X D H F C O O L Q I O P E
D B A D Q V E O C M F L C O L
R L E F C B D H X K Q S C Y U
S M C J O R F Z B H E K E U U
L L A B T O O F A R V Y R I Q
S P O R T S B C N J F Q B P K
```

We hope you've enjoyed learning some of the secrets of Washington, DC. We've filled the book with loads of information. But the city's neighborhoods are crammed with interesting places and stories. Tour our nation's capital and start uncovering secrets of your own!

If you enjoyed *Secrets of our Nation's Capital*, check out *Secrets of the National Parks*, *Secrets of Disneyland*, and *Secrets of Walt Disney World*!

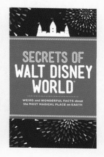